At the Heart of a Lotus

AT THE HEART OF A

Lotus

Raisaunya "Starr" Jones

At the Heart of a Lotus
Copyright © 2019 by Raisaunya Jones

ISBN 13: 978-0-578-50817-7

Dedication

FIRST; To God, for keeping me, for leading me and for providing for me. Without YOU, none of this would be possible.

This book is dedicated to my Grandma who held onto these letters from my heart. She pushed me to release them because she felt like there were other young girls who could relate to my story.

To my God mom who pushed me for 10 years to follow my dreams. She never gave up on me and was there every step of the way in this process.

Lastly: To every guy who hurt me, helped me, and loved me, thank you for these experiences; without them, I may not have found myself.

Introduction: At the Heart of a Lotus

I was muddy...dirty...untouched and in a dark place for what seemed like ages. My cries were silent. When my mother discovered my gift of writing I was 13 and had already attempted suicide twice. My father was incarcerated. My mother was dying but she needed me to survive.

Without my parents I was left to raise four boys and myself. I missed a lot of school and spent a lot of countless nights washing clothes, doing the grocery shopping, making dinner and cleaning. Life was exhausting.

I started writing at a young age as a way to escape, an opportunity to share my truth and a way to heal. I had a lot on my mind and on my heart with no one to talk to. Any time I felt something that I couldn't verbalize I wrote it down.

I have always loved to paint pictures with my words. I wrote and kept my letters together but I never intended to release them. My grandmother gave me all my poems one day and said, "You need to share these with the world because there is a young girl out there who needs to hear this, who needs to know she's not alone."

I entitled this book *At the Heart of a Lotus* because I viewed myself as a flower. I am beautiful, sometimes unnoticed and sometimes weak in bad weather (bad circumstances).

When I am watered, nurtured and cared for I become strong; life and vibrancy is added to me. I learned that the flower of my zodiac sign (Cancer) is a lotus flower; and when I began to do research I fell in love with the symbolism. The way a lotus grows is symbolic of how we transcend through our lives.

The lotus flower is a symbol of strength. It grows from muddy waters. It arises at the sunrise, untouched by the darkness and the soil. The deeper the mud, the more beautiful the flower grows. It learns lessons and becomes self-aware. The more resilient we become by growing through our experiences, the more beautiful we turn out to be.

Every new experience I gained gave me a new petal. My trials were the mud that I had to grow through with resilience. These are the spiritual reflections of a poet about friendship, heartbreak, and love. *At the Heart of a Lotus* is the tale of a young girl who shares her experiences through love, friendship, spirituality, and heartbreak, in order to reach her sunlight.

I hope that you are able to see the picture I painted on each line as a reminder that you are not alone in the journey of life.

Starr

At the Heart of a Lotus
Contents

Spirituality and Self Awareness

In God I Trust

Growing up in this world
Since I was a little girl
I had to learn independence
From all of the older women
I grew up on the streets so I know life
I used to listen to my neighbor beatin' up on
his wife
It's been 11 years my dad has been in jail, and
now my moms is dead...
I have nightmares at night every time I lay my
head
Which really isn't that often
Since I saw her in that coffin
But the one thing she taught me is:
"You don't need any man to live
It doesn't matter if you're alone
You CAN make it out here on your own
Remember this, cause it's a must:
Always say 'In God I trust'
He will give you what you need to live
And the advice I give you, give your kids!"
I do what I got to do
That way I know I'll make it through
I've learned that the only man I need for love,
Is my Father, my Savior, the Lord above

Colors of My Skin

My friend said to me once, "I love you because you're there for me and you care. When I need someone to talk to, you're always there. I love that we can hang out for hours and do nothing. You're my best friend and I know it's true, however I have a confession I have to share with you. I have insecurity that I hide within my soul. I feel like flipping out sometimes, and over it I have no control. Sometimes I feel so ugly and I wonder why I do. So I mirror how I feel and turn it around on you.

I tell you that I hate you because I don't like my reflection. The only reason why I say this is because of your complexion."

I told her, "All my life I have been picked on because of how I look. Treated like a criminal, a dirty ugly crook. People pulled my hair, poked me and asked how I got so light. They would call me 'little white girl' or the most famous one, 'light bright.' I didn't choose to be this way, but this is who I am. When it comes to being a good person I do the best that I can. You pick up a book and judge it before you get the chance to read; the contents in between the lines are truly what you need."

With tears she told me, "I need someone to hold me, your skin gets you attention, sometimes I crave to have. People your complexion tend to treat people really bad. But it's not you, I promise, so let's not hate each other. I love what's in your heart, I just don't like your color."

I explained to her, "Tha
t's a stereotype, girl and you know it, if you are playing with me you really need to show it. I really love you girl but don't put us in a category. We are all the same color; our skin just tells a different story. It represents the beauty that our ancestors glorified. It lets us know our history looking into each other's eyes. It should help us to relate and push away from a debate. How the world changed us to segregate from each other I will never understand. Since you are the one doing it, maybe you can.

Wait until you get to know me, don't judge me by my skin. What you see outside is no match to what's within."

Reality Check

Always I had been
Afraid to even be your friend
Alas my heart began to mend when my fears
came to an end

We would walk around and talk at night
At those moments I always thought I might
open up to you
But it was another fear, what should I do?
The truth is, I am still afraid of you
        Afraid of the things you will say
        Afraid of the things you will do

I feel that life is not ready for you but you
don't care
We share everything, our most intimate fears
and I learned to like you

Everyone's always judging me asking who I'd
rather be
I don't know because I am calm, discreet and
friendly

You are loud, outspoken and mean see; people
don't like you but I have to

Now my next step with you is a must; I have to
learn to give you my trust
Because you see
You are me.

The Voice Within

People often try so hard to fit in but they never
listen to their voice within
They change the way they act and dress just to
see who it will impress

When they don't get attention, they get upset
I personally don't see why they let things like
that get to their head while it haunts their sleep
as they lie in bed
The next day they call their friends and
complain, that the "want to be cool" with
people who were calling them names

The friend on the phone tries to figure it out
and wonders what their friend is talking about
The confidant friend finally gets a clue, she
says, "The only person that matters is you. It
really doesn't matter what they say about your
clothes. Who cares what they say about your
legs and your nose? If you like who you are
then everything is cool. Show everyone that
and they'll feel like fools.

If you love you, spread love and hope
Then what can they say? You're ugly?
Nope!
God is beautiful and you're beautiful too; if it
helps, I want to say that I love you!"
Her friend feels better and the magic begins,
she taught her to listen to the voice within.

My Demands

I woke up one day and demanded that you
respect me but, you ignored me
it was just so odd of a request
This was the first time in years that you've
known me to ask of such a thing;
something like this isn't what you'd EXPECT
for me to want from you
You have seen me gallantly flaunting around
in my body con print dress enticing your stare
and arousing your sense...s....

I. Am. Not. A. Ho.

I just call it free spirited, but I've learned that
free spirits are looked down upon

SO because I choose to be comfortable in my
flesh and the way that I choose to dress
somehow means that I am allowing you to
gawk.
Giving you permission to flock.
I am not a science show.
I am not a piece of meat or display for you to
cop a feel.
Yes, it is amazing.
Yes, you can stare.
But do not touch.
Don't ever tell me I'm "doing too much"
I'm doin ME!....like you wish you could....

Skin and All Its Glory

                                    Light skin
                        Dark skin
              All skin...

Core of sensational thoughts
Shadow of the night chocolate deep as the
ocean; I swim in the mysteriousness of the
origin its crazy oh, the thoughts I've been
thinking... skin sunshine bright, spicy like
espanol, so smooth la color es muy bonito...
just looking at light...
skin makes me want to flamenco into another
world with people of all skins

Latino, African, Caucasian, bi-racial; beautiful!
Different kinds, so many unique beings it
reflects what's on the inside.

If your heart is beautiful
your skin will be beautiful
you'll be beautiful too.

True Values of Life

A wise man once told me that if you know that
there is at least one person that loves you then
it's enough

But it's tough

When you've got heartache and problems and
they can't help you solve them; you're on their
time and don't want to become a burden or a
pest
So you give it a rest and end up feeling lonely

Yes of course they can give you advice
And tell you what's right
But how do you truly know?
Then when that person is gone you have
nowhere to turn
but up
you must have forgotten there's always one
who will love you regardless

That wise man also told me that I should never
let anybody hold me back from getting my
spot in heaven or to get the chance to meet my
one true love.

Analytical Mind

Observant of the tides; of waves, of the stars
within the skies
Interested in life and in truth; in hair, teeth and
in eyes
To touch the hands of others and feel upon
their skin
To want to know the answer before the
problem begins
To listen to the words of others and analyze the
situation
From babies and birds and sunsets, to fall in
love with evolution
To want to save the world and want to do it all
alone
To grow up living crazy then give it a different
meaning and make it all your own
To stand in front of a mirror and examine all
you see
Every crease, every mole and every flaw
everything that makes up me
From my freckles to my baby teeth to my little
baby toes
All these things go on in my mind, things that
no one even knows
To love the world in every perspective and
respect natural beauty
I love it because it's real and a part of it is me...

Who Am I?

I have always wanted people to recognize me
for who I really am
I wish they could understand that I try the best
that I can
I try not to mess up and I try to help out,
isn't that enough?

You can't just accept the fact that no one is
perfect, we all have flaws?
We are all beautiful, God created us all equal
Maybe you can do things better than me,
that won't help your personality

I have a great heart
I have got great morals
If you really knew me
instead of looking through me you would
know who I am

I am: an artist, a poet, a chocolate FIEND
A girl with a great sense of humor who just
happens to look mean,
a Chris Brown fan who loves to read books

I am not like another girl, strung out over her
looks,
I'm an energetic,
sensitive,
timid,
wild child and I refuse to change

"The industrious One" is the true meaning of
my name
I am who I am,
that is who I will be
to sum it all up;
I am a unique creation of the LORD,

L-O-R-D.

Only You Know the Answer

I find myself asleep at peace, then suddenly
awoke and in the midst
of gangs and drugs and pregnant teens

Someone help me...what is this?
Blue, red, black and white, all segregated
what's the meaning?
The blood of your brother, forever stained on
your name, learn from the teachings

I'm running and yelling, there's something
behind me, but it won't take off its mask
It's reaching for me, scary, horrific, trying to
hold me in its grasp
"Let go!" I hide and watch the old folks travel
in the cold by foot
No buses, high gas rates, it seems this isn't at
all good
They shiver and shake as they watch youth
destroy each other one by one
Sometimes they feel the glory but the war is
not quite done
I'm discovered by the mystery and still the
chase goes on
Running through a holy garden, and yet, the
beauty is all gone.
Inside myself, I hear a voice demanding that I
slow down

Before I knew it, my world was dark, and I was
lying on the ground,
I forced myself up, gained my composure, but,
I was chilling to the core
I decide to forget, but when I turned, I was
standing in a war
Brave soldiers were fighting for our rights
Afraid, yet brave, they are fighting for our
LIVES.
I have put on army gear; I am afraid and I
don't know what to do.

The voice again, "You have got to do it, we are
counting on you."
"NO!" I break free from my personal
imprisonment
I break down and cry.
"I don't know if I can do this…!"
The voice just told me, "Try. You'll never know
if you are capable if you don't believe in you. If
you give it effort, there is nothing you can't do.
Think of the others who are always there for
you. Be yourself, have strength and courage, it
will help you to get through. In the end, you're
all you'll have; alone, complete your tasks."

When the mystery was finished, it slowly took
off its mask.
If I would have paid attention and learned
from what I was taught, I would have known it
was my main supporter,
How funny, it was GOD.

King of Hearts

There are…52 cards in a deck. As a child I would always divide them by hearts, diamonds, spades or clovers. Maybe to see if the number had changed. My favorite was the hearts, they seemed prettier to me at the time…(chuckles).

I lived life like my deck of cards; always looking for luck. The number four, the clover I mean. But to no avail, ya' know so I gave up and as I grew older I made friends and lost as many as the spades in the deck. I felt as though I had a spade in my back for every time they crossed the line, lied, or tried to deceive me.

Hurtful teenagers, boy I tell ya.

My deck of hearts though. I was careful about that. (Ha, ha) I pretended as if I would give away one but if I continued to give them out I would end up with none.

I had decided to keep the queen for myself. I hid the king. I figured I would give it to the guy most worthy of having it. Since I am the queen, he would be my king. (smile)

I hid it so well I forgot where I hid it. I got older and as the years passed I kept ... losing ... cards…. and then one day I realized I only had one left…the ace. I got more cautious than before.

I hadn't even realized I was running out of hearts. I had given diamonds to the real GOOD guys, the ones I couldn't afford to give a heart to but wanted them to know they were SPECIAL.

I knew I was close to being out of those and some of my hearts HAD been stolen. It left me teary eyed so many nights because every time I felt like I had lost a piece of me. I would pick myself back up and keep it moving.

Now I was stuck with this guy and this...one...card. We talked, walked and went out. It took a while for me to let down my guard, but I thought, Hey, this guy is LEGIT." (SHRUGS SHOULDERS)

When he said those three words I hesitated, waited awhile before I said it back. Then I did. But I wasn't sure. Time went by and he grew on me. Lol, it was awesome. I had decided to give him my last card. I just knew it was time. He kept it and he took care of it.

Until... I hate that word until...I noticed he was changing...I went into where he kept the card and I saw it was fading but I just couldn't UNDERSTAND. I left for some time to handle academic business and we began to argue. Things just were not as they seemed.

Then on the day of love...Valentine's Day I came to visit and when I looked at the card again...my ace of hearts...it had deteriorated...

That's how I knew that my ace was no longer my ace. I dreamed and cried that I could just find that one last card that I had LOST. I became depressed...and I could not

FUNCTION. I decided it was time for me to go back to church. I had no other options or answers.

Time and time again I began to feel better. Then one night as I stood in the pew I felt a shift. I felt it go through my body, through my soul; but my mind couldn't grasp it.

I came to and felt someone grab me by the shoulder gently. In their hand was my last card. My king of hearts. I was joyful. I boasted...." Man I thought I lost this!!!"

The man in front of me said, "No, you didn't lose it. You gave it to Me years ago and strayed away from Me. You went from person to person who destroyed your heart when you gave it to them. I have come to show you that I have cared for your heart all of this time and I continue to do so, even if you decide to STRAY from Me again."

He stuck the card in his shirt pocket and turned to walk away. I felt like I had known Him forever but for some reason His name was not coming to me. He turned back to embrace me and I knew it was Him. The man I had longed for, for so many years WAS RIGHT HERE. I couldn't believe it.

While in His arms I whispered..." I love you Jesus."

He said..." I LOVE YOU MORE."

I smiled and said, "I know."

You're Beautiful Baby...But....

It burns my soul that one day I might have to explain to my daughter that she cannot be free.

"No baby you can't wear that."
When she asks why she will see the fire in my eyes, "Baby, you can't wear that because somebody may think that because you have this on that it's okay to touch you...that you're saying okay to your privacy being invaded and I don't want you to take this the wrong way because YOU'RE BEAUTIFUL BABY BUT you can't wear that."

 When she says, "Mom, I don't know what you mean."
I will just have to say, "Baby you're a QUEEN, but the society we live in will JUDGE YOU although wearing this makes you happy you have to find happiness in another form of freedom to avoid being sexualized
and objectified
and taunted and teased...
baby please...
don't wear that...this isn't Africa...it ain't the West Indies...where you can walk around bare foot and naked or dance freely and be happy...no baby; this is America 'the land of the free' supposedly."
When she says, "But mommy, are we free?"

19

I will have no answer, "Just say baby you are
beautiful but, you have to cover up. You just
can't show too much or else they may label
you a 'slut.' This is what was said to me...
I was told I wasn't allowed to be free because
of how I was built someone invaded my
privacy and they didn't feel any guilt...
Baby girl, you are beautiful... but protect
yourself.
Watch out...cause what I am sayin' is true...
I am trying to protect you, because I don't
want what they did to me to happen to you..."

I Am

I am too tired...
I am too stressed...
I am too woke
I am too blessed!
I am, too, the kingdom
I am too, next
I am too unfearful
Never settling for less.
I am too, Sandra
I am too, Tray
I am too, changing
I AM the future yet, today
I am too, the voices
I am too, silence
I am too, speaking
I am too, timeless
I am too, struggle...
YET, I am too faithful
I am too, tears
Because I am too, GRATEFUL.

Nkd

Nakedness is beautiful, nakedness is freedom. I want to live in a world with like-minded people stripped of clothes and fears where we can talk about realms and not judge about the clothes on our backs or shoes on our feet...do you see me?

I want to be completely natural; no mac.

Swimsuits aren't enough for me. I want to not be fearful of being bare.
I want to be comfortable being free...and you haven't begun to see me if you've only seen me without clothes...Will you strip for me?
I mean...beyond the external layers of what the eye can see; I want to SEE you.
I want to know...YOU.
Let me hear you in the silence, and feel you in the dark.
Get rid of what society has conditioned us to see...and believe.
Who ARE we?
We are ROYAL. Royal...
but ONLY when we are naked.

In To Me I See (Intimacy)

You were but a piece of my journey.
My beginning to an enlightened segment.

Ascension.

It was never intended to be a physical thing.
It became physical once our souls wanted to
get closer together to become whole; the left to
my right, the yin to my yang in search of each
other-intertwined...you were my muse.
And the burning heat of desire became
pressure.

The universe knows my kryptonite.
A dick. I mean a-dict-tion.

When I met you my spirit had already known
you; my spirit already felt at home IN you.

My twin flame- we spoke in nonverbal so
when we opened our mouths to speak; it often
led to miscommunication and distraction
because our vessels were trying to convey a
different message than our spirits needed us to
hear, and learn and see.

With our minds eye.
We were only ever meant to be **mirrors**.
To be one and *inner*stand.

However, biology took over and the hormonal,
overloaded capacity of the flesh made us...
made me...weak.
How risky.
How often we lie TO each other,
so we can lie IN each other
and then lie BY each other never speaking
truth but still knowing.
Because...our spirits can't lie.
Intuitively reading each other's thoughts and
feelings without intention through each
passionate embrace our heart spoke of
subconscious fears and heartbreak

Of deadlines and discrepancies
We saw each other with our eyes closed
Heard each other with our minds closed.
How could we feel each other with our hearts
closed?

Who knows?
Maybe because WE had no intentions of ever
opening them.
UNBEKNOWNST TO US - it was always about
love.
Of forgiveness.
Of others.
Of God.
Of growth.
Of self-realization.
Esteem…. Of self.

At the Heart of a Lotus

At the heart of a Lotus you will find a light
dimming.
You will find
memories of past transgressions and pain.
Deeper and closer to the core the fears of
trauma that haunts me.

Who would ever abuse such a beautiful and
delicate flower? To try and take away the
essence of her femininity before she had a
chance to fully bloom.

In the dark all of this comes to light.
In the dark, all of the mud surrounds me.
In the dark, I feel the raindrops on my petals as
the tears fall on my cheeks and seep through
my mouth
I try to open it to scream,
nothing comes out.

So I sit...and I wait. Until day break.
I wait for the light to come back again.
The darkness was symbolic of my pain
Over time, I have realized how much
HEALING is done in the dark. Although
invisible to the human eye,
GOD STILL SEES ME.
You may forget about me because you see me
covered in my mess, but as I bloom into the

light I become stronger, more beautiful, and fuller than you could ever imagine!

Because....you failed to see...through all of the mess that is my flaws.
The mess that is my trauma.

I come out resilient, undamaged — that IS what I am!

I am the Lotus and AT THE HEART you will find my strength to persevere,
        strength to bloom amongst the chaos,
        strength to love through the pain,
        strength to prevail from the heartache.

There is GOD within ME.

Lessons of Life

Look, Love, Listen, Learn

Different people — different lives
Through tribulations and hard trials
All trying to figure out what's right
Stop, think!

I've thought about what to do and I think
about what to say but when I think about
opening up, I end up in disarray

The conclusion is confusion
Within our diffusion, I'm losing in this battle
called life
I am watching everything, and I am watching
everyone

I am seeing that the healing is still not done
I see that the war is still not won
Life has just begun
The explanation as to why I'm pacing back and
forth in my mind,
is because my thoughts intertwine like serpents
Criminal acts of desertion toward my heart
have left my soul torn apart because we lack
the knowledge to **look**

Down the street you see a young man on the
corner
Gunshots and drug spots
Another mother mourns
WHY?

I knew a young man, tried to grab him by the
hand, tried to show him the right life
But he felt it wasn't right
Enough for him
After his rehabilitation he didn't take into
consideration that things might get better
Some day
Some way
If we just look deeper and learn to **love**...

Now that's a subject that we forgot to mention
Now we will bring to your attention
Another issue that plagues our communities
and dismantles our unities is not only our drug
rate
But the pregnancies that we accommodate
This is directed towards the ladies and the
guys; love is in the soul not within the hips or
the eyes
Love one another as sister, brother, father, and
mother

<u>Stop killing</u>

Because death brings heartache and pain
Just like using love in vain
Don't pay attention to words,
Pay attention to the feeling
That is the only way you will know if it's real
Yeah!
Ladies, there are those nights when he holds
you nice and tight

And you know the moments right, but if you
examine his composure
And he does not offer any closure how can you
be sure?
But when he says he loves you
And then he says he loves her
Unconditional? I think not sir.

Protect yourself
Or just stop and **listen** to your heart
It never lies
This is what I've learned
Sometimes I feel like dying
And sometimes I feel like crying
But I know if I stay strong I'll live long enough
to conquer my dreams
And though sometimes it seems as if the world
is dire but I can do it, with my friends and my
family, I can get through it.

If I just look at the world, love myself, listen to
my heart, and learn from my experiences
I can do anything.

A Change Begins with You

Although I'm not done living,
I've lived a lot of life and I know about strife
I know I have rights
Such as freedom of speech
Now I'm willing to speak about the struggles
that I've witnessed not just throughout my
own, but in other people's lives

Now just take a second to breathe
And take a moment to grieve over the lost
souls of the deceased that were a cause of the
streets
And in the homes of our beloved, the dearly
departed
Who's names have been engraved on our
hearts with tears, whose memories will be
stained on our brains for years but over what?
Words?

She heard she said this.
He heard he said that.
People you think are your friends constantly
stabbing you in the back.
Listen to this, we always tell our friends
someone is wrong for being fake but you
contradict yourself and your next words are
rooted in hate.
Believe what you say for if you do the same
thing it makes you a hypocrite, a fraud;
Believe in God for He is the truth

Or it could be because of little corner hustling
thugs who believe that's the only way to get
ahead in life
…Yeah right...

When you really think about it these two go
hand in hand because words twists into lies
and this causes trouble within the eyes of the
dealer who most likely knows many killers
Who don't care about your life

Think about this: if we just take these words
and turn them around we could get what we
deserve; respect.
Respect for one another can broaden into all of
our sisters and brothers
Slow down the pace and embrace everybody
who is willing
No, but because of the fear of being hurt in the
arms of love we're still killing; however, the
change can begin with you.

Now this may sound kind of funny
But trust me I'm not a dummy
We have all been there… the times we have
spent in the dark with our constant tears
bottled up and tightened and of course you
may get frightened
But let it out or if shaken you may explode

There's always somebody around to
understand

Someone who's never afraid to offer a hand
There's always someone lurking, struggling
with addiction, pressure, misery or grief
 but if you have the belief that anything is
possible, then anything REALLY is.

A Cry for Help

Confusing mind games,
trapped in this maze called life.
Every movement, every word must be precise.
Should I listen to my mind, or should I listen to
my heart?
I'm invisible to the fact that my so-called love
will be torn apart.
Should I pay attention to my tears; river
flowing down my face?
Should I stand back, when I can win this
lifelong race?

Should I listen to my soul or pay attention to
the voices?
Listen to what makes me stronger to make
wiser choices?
Bottle up my secrets and dispose of them like
trash?
Focus on my future or be concerned about the
past?
Wonder about tomorrow when today is not
quite done?
Should I try to finish something that has only
just begun?
Walk around in sadness, when joy lives deep
inside me?
Set up and get right all my main priorities?
Should I organize my life or leave myself a
cluttered mess?

Sit down and pay attention, to myself, Should I
confess?
Try to make a difference or leave the world to
rot?
Wonder to myself should I, which I admit I do
a lot.
Shoot the gun or put it down...help me, which
one is right?
The biggest choice I'll ever have to make
        is to choose between death and life.

Pay Attention

I walk around with my friends and I pay
attention to the things around me

I closely listen to the sounds and voices that
surround me
I overhear conversations from those on cell
phones
13 year-olds screaming "I'm grown!"
But I think, just because you have a child on
your hip and money in your jeans
If you can't support yourself or that child what
do those words really mean?
Are you paying attention?

I have uncles and cousins influenced by drugs
Got middle school boys thinking they're thugs
Little girls wishing and praying for one
affectionate hug,
Pay attention!
People think it's dumb to sit and enjoy a book,
instead they flaunt their looks
Apple bottom jeans and timberland shoes
Don't waste your money child, go buy a clue
The most beautiful and respected thing lives
inside of you
Your heart

Are you paying attention?

I remember when my neighbor beat his wife
and in front of their children threatened to take
her life
I wonder what they thought when they saw
those tears
The thought of that moment has haunted me
for years

Some people think violence is the key but
that's foul
And because of it most have, or will go to trial
for a sentence they didn't think they would
have to serve
Some are serving for something they don't
deserve

If the world was right
You wouldn't have to fight for your life or
your rights
You'd be innocent until proven guilty, instead
of guilty until proven innocent

Are you paying attention?

This is life.
This is real! I'm just explaining how I feel.

I thank my mom for showing me what's right
and explaining how to move on in life
I thank the Lord for allowing me to live
and for giving me the blessing of being able to
envision and pay attention.

When the Last Tear Drops

When the last tear drops...
Heavy breathing...fast paced
Blood is pumping heart race...(ing) in the dark
at the dead of the night
Praying to a God to save his life
A life full of robbing, killing and chaos
Not caring about the consequences only
concerned about the payoff
And always running. Never getting anywhere
Having the title of a "G," so he couldn't hold
any fear
But he's still running and now he hears the
shots
He wasn't quick enough, "POP! POP! POP!"
When the last tear drops....

Pain piercing through her back...excruciating...
All of a sudden she is wearing the food she
was making...
Dissatisfaction...emotionally shattering...
Along the walls and rugs her blood is deeply
splattered
Swelling, whelps and bruising a black eye
upon her face
Hearing words of torment trying to put her in
her place
At the bottom...no feeling of self-worth
The more he digs into her the more it hurts
He smacks her then she blacks out,
"THUD!" her body drops

Domestic violence has always been the case
whether she wanted it or not..
When the last tear drops...

She laid down her head and opened up a can
of sin
Deep secrets of her life
She never let anyone in,
Every night she got on her knees and begged
the Lord to keep her sane
In her mind she flashes back to the night she
screamed his name in vain
Now she reaps the repercussion of her life
changing decisions

People always tried to warn her but she never
listened
A different guy every week, to her it was all
just a game
Until someone asked her, 'What is to be the
baby's name?"
And then inside her womb she felt a kick
She made the decision, "I'm not keeping it"
The baby's life or mine, I've got too much
going on
I want to go to college, will my decision be
wrong
On her face was an appalling contortion
She cried as she said, "I'm getting an abortion."
When the last tear drops...

Overcome Your Fears

My heart speaks, my heart cries
My soul sleeps where my secrets lie
Sometimes the world drops bombs on us and
we try so hard to ignore the pain which we all
have inside
We never release what we think when the time
comes
We've got people dying, babies crying, the
world that I'm in, is so stuck in its ways
It doesn't look beyond what is right in front it
Best friends and enemies, people we don't
know and everyone we do is going through so
much pain

I feel like dropping to my knees and giving my
tears to the devil, asking the Lord for mercy,
"Why have I been inflicted with so much
pain?"

The feeling I endure, when I hear a man calling
his queen a whore;
marking her body with black and blue
making her go through what he went through
in his past

As a people we need to rise above pain
Pain hurts, but it wasn't created to bring us joy
Find different ways to release it

My thesis is this: pain comes in different ways;
we never know when it's going to come; there
is no way you can run from it
Look it in the face and know that you are
stronger
It may not go away in an instant but at least
you'll know you can deal with pain

Context Clues of Life

I walk through school just as free as I please
I walk toward the door and feel the cool breeze
The birds are chirping all while the sun shines
There's no life on earth as beautiful as mine
There's lemonade in the yard, I pour a glass
I've forgotten my shoes and I can feel the grass
Underneath my feet... I love the feel
Sometimes I can't believe it's real
I hear voices inside so that's where I go
I see my children; they seem to be grown
They laugh, they shout they have a great time
They talk about the news and the latest crimes
I shout "Hi" but they don't even hear
I say it louder but it's like I'm not there
They walk right past me and right out the door
I turn around and stare at the four
I am appalled but my daughter, my first, my
miracle blessing is missing
I ask, "Where's your sister?"
But they walk away, to me they're making the
worst out of a beautiful day
They walk down the street towards a cemetery
They stop at a grave that says my name
I think to myself, "This must be a game"
All of a sudden I see a bright flash of my past
Before me are parts of my life:
I'm with my beautiful children,
I am a wonderful wife
I fall to my knees because here I am all alone
There's a ghost in this place...and it's my own.

A Cry for Compassion

She smokes half a dutch just to reach her
escape
Trying to run from the pain and agony of being
raped
Her tears fall like a rainstorm, her thoughts
swarm like a tsunami
In her dreams she screams "I need you, please
help me. Mommy!
 Where are you?" She wakes up to realize her
mom was beaten again
by that needle and coke she withdraws to
...what she believes to be her friend

Listen to her silent cries
Deep within her anger lies
But no one hears them...

"You gonna do this for us homie?"
They put a gun in his hands; he holds the steel
tight within his grip
They want him to show his appreciation and
put the stain of another man's blood on his
tender fingertips
He didn't have a voice, he didn't have a choice
They helped him...gave him what he asked for
In return he got rid of who they blamed for
their gang war
"Pop. Pop. Pop. Pop. Pop!"
 Now he's sitting in the court room with the
jury and the judge

Recollecting what happened, the little boy
inside him budged
when they said, "We find him guilty.", he
knew all hope was gone
His mother yelled out, "Oh Lord, help my
baby!"
Her son was praying for the Lord to help her
all along
She hadn't paid the bills in months
he had to find a way
If only she knew that the $20K she got in the
mail came from him killing that day

He got locked away but nobody cared to ask
what made him do it, or why
No one stopped to think that maybe as a guy,
he had more reasons to cry

No one listens to our stories; no one sees our
tears of pain
Everyone thinks we have issues and we are all
just playing games throwing our lives away
because we are stubborn, but the truth is
that this is the only way
When we try to tell them the truth they turn
and walk away
But people...we need you...
We need you to listen to us...guide us...lead us
in the right direction
Because this life we live is corrupted totally
filled with imperfection

No matter how much we try to explain it or if
we scream at the top of our lungs
The only response we get, "you'll get it when
you're older, right now you're much too
young"
But we do get it. Do you?

A young boy was roaming the streets one night
He left his home because his mother and father
were having a fight
He had been looking for a job but no one
would accept him
It seemed as if no one really cared about the
outcome of the family, except him
His younger sister, the doctors said, was to die
within a couple of years
She was his best friend, losing her was one of
his biggest fears
He saw a lady walking, he ran and snatched
her purse
As he ran towards home, the confusion ate at
him, but the guilt felt worse
He checked through her wallets and he found
out where she lived
He realized he was friends with one of her kids
When he went to return it, the lady asked him,
"Why?"
Right there on her front stoop...he broke down
and cried
He said, "I know what I did and I know it
wasn't right; I just thought that if I had more
money I could help save her life.

No one knows how I feel waking up and going
to bed without a meal
No one knows the things I go through; they
don't understand how I feel
Do you know how it feels to be beaten because
your family doesn't like you?
They do things just to spite you
Do you know how it feels to never feel loved?"

The lady took him in her arms and said "I do.
But robbing is not right, I really wish I could
help you."

He wiped his face and said, "Some people
believe that crime is not the answer; but the
real reason I did it was to try and pay for my
sister's treatment for brain cancer."

Trauma will drive someone insane
Torment every nerve in their brain
But some will say that we are to blame
How?
We are just following what we see
Misery loves company, you see
If someone...
anyone...
just listened and helped us through hard times
They would see that our need for affection and
attention is the reason behind these crimes...

Knowledge Inheritance

How come we live on these poverty stricken
streets and Bush's campaign promises are
some we never see?
Growing up
I had it tough
But I made it the best with what I had
I was even fortunate enough to have a
relationship with my dad
Though the man is behind bars he is trying to
live his life right
Just like the other millions of men, he won't
give up without a fight
Every time I get those 15 minute talks
With my pops, he drops some knowledge
about the environment that surrounds us

We talk about racism and sexism
We scope every topic like, why is it that I gotta
sit in church and hear police sirens going past?
How come I want to be somebody who just
wants to help people but I have to learn math?

He can't explain why in basketball
big girls get picked last... or never at all
I tell him my thoughts on politics and we
compare our views
He tries to explain to me why a Christian life is
the right life to choose
I get the male point of view of a female

He never holds back and gives me all the
details
We talk about the times he had with his
homeboy Tone
I remember it sitting here now it all plays back
minute after minute every second so clear
oh how I wish my Uncle Tone was still here
that memory is something I hold dear after his
funeral they said I'd never have to attend
another funeral but almost ten years later I had
to go to his sister's: my mom's
when asked just how this phases me I answer
so calm
why should I be mad? You want me to walk
around sad
 I'm glad she's gone and I miss her but I don't
wish this life on nobody, its hard but we got to
deal with it
they say love is pain
you gotta wait for the sunshine after the rain
if this is true then I don't want to feel it...do
you?
my father always tells me this same message
I'll share
God never gives us more than we can bear
no matter what always care about who you are
and always share love, have peace be proud
and stand tall and through everything you go
through, give it your all.
Man...I love my dad...

Bridge Over Troubled Water

I go to school.
Do my work.
read my books
hit the sheets.
& in my dreams I see everything going on in
them streets.

You. . .
Wake and bake.
Serve ya work and run the streets.

We
Are different. . .but yet the same.

See. . . I know the game
My daddy went through it, his daddy too
Had an uncle who was using; my auntie was
too
I reminisce about when I had to go to my
favorite uncle's funeral at the age of four
cause....
they found him on Flowers Ave covered in
blood...shot him in the back...who does
somebody like that?

then years later...
another fallen soldier in what used to be my
favorite place...
I can still visualize his face in the park by the
pool…

these fools...
wish I could build a bridge so I can get over
my troubles...
but every time I try the trauma doubles...
"homies cuh"...I learned that young.
the code of conduct, our "swear to GOD"
them's ya peoples for life, the ones you never
cross...mhm. yea.
I get it. family right???
family wouldn't shoot my cousin...least I don't
think they would
family couldn't rob one another... at least...I
don't think they could
family wouldn't snitch, family wouldn't lie...
family couldn't hurt you or kill your blood and
still look you in the eye
at least...I don't think they would
year...after year...crime ...after crime...
we count the number of times...FAMILY wasn't
protected.
we watch our backs at all times cause
unloyalty was detected.
it's a shame but it's true... you so addicted to
the streets.. but the streets ain't addicted to you
the streets got no commitment to you
whatsoever see
the streets will sit there and watch you bleed...
for hours...maybe days...damn them streets
and their selfish ways..
but yet and still...we love' em...
we all grew up together right....
but that ain't what we remember every night...

all ya'll wanna do is fight...
so many I lost...
I wish I could press rewind
cause after I lost my mom . . .
if I lose another I might lose my mind
I'm 20!!! & I lost... my daddy...
2 aunts...1 uncle...and cousins...
Some jailed, wounded and others put to rest
now the next generation is being put to the test
their test-tosterone is getting the best of them
what...can we do??
all the ish that we been through...
haha...you must have forgot...n*gga I know
you
and you, and you...yea! &YOU!
we all older so the tears and frustration have
canceled out our memories of laughter
eff a happily ever after...
cause the streets robbed us of all of
them...right...
this is what I think of every night...
right before I…
wake up,
go to school,
 do my work,
read my books,
then again hit the sheets.
wondering who's the next one to be taken from
me by the damn streets.

damn shame.

a year after this poem was written, I lost my brother to gun violence. Rest in Peace Antwaun Hasaun Leake.

AT THE HEART OF A

Lotus

Lessons in Friendship

Got A Great Friend

Great friends are hard to come by
And when you're with them times seem to fly
You always confide in each other
Like big sister or big brother
But something totally different
The chemistry there is so apparent
Sometimes you might not get along
But that doesn't last very long
You forget about that lousy fight
Talking on the phone the next night
If you've got a great friend stick by their side
Let them know you're in for the long ride
That no matter what, when, how or where
You're always gonna be there
You're friends that never say never
That's why you'll be friends forever

There's something I want you to know
That no matter what or where you go
I've got you're back through thick and thin
Cause in me you've got a great friend

Our Phone Calls

We are always talking
Recapping the day's events
From day break until the nights
We talk about each other we laugh and clown
around
And when we are having a bad day we sit and
we don't make any sounds
When I'm crying or they're hurting we can feel
each other's pain
We think so much alike it's like we share the
same brain
We never talk about the past; the present is all
we speak of
We never recap on what we went through,
never speak on when we shared love
But it's cool because our phone calls let me
know
When they refuse to let their feelings show
In my mind I let them go
In my heart this was not so
I was fighting against feeling like this again
Because I hate being in love with the guy I call
my best friend

How to Deal

It's hard to be yourself with obstacles in your
way
Even harder when everyone's got something to
say
To walk around in happiness when everyone
else is sad
They do this purposely just to make you mad
Will you let it get to you?
It's hard to speak truthfully when all you know
is lies
How shameful people are to lie while staring
into your eyes
To take your love when their plan is to abuse it
To use the word "love" when they don't know
how to use it
It's hard to care for everyone else when you're
not sure if they care for you
The feelings they portray are false not even
pretending to be true
How hard is it to know what's wrong and not
try to make it right?
Even harder it is to be able to but not take
control of your life
Life is confusing and painful when you don't
know how to deal
And the hardest thing to accomplish is how to
not be fake, but real

Where Do Tears Come From?

Where do tears come from?
The heavy drops of water that fall and make
my vision blurry
That stem from my emotions of pain,
happiness and fury
The evidence my body shows
To let the entire world know
That I'm going through some things at the time
And the sound of a muffled cry is mine
My tears
Often afraid to show
That everlasting flow
That I allow to be welled up inside and along
the corridors of my thoughts
For I shall not let anyone ever see me
distraught
But I'm hurting
Still yet, I smile through my agony and laugh
at all their jokes
If I laugh and listen, on my tears, I think I'll
choke
But in my loneliness I let my mind soar
And close the door
To any outsiders who I feel would be
concerned
Because to hide my tears from them is
something I haven't learned
I let it out until I feel it's enough and okay to
face reality

But there are so many waiting that saw
through my act... and me
I spun around wondering, so upset and getting
colder
But a friend amidst the crowd around me
holds out a hand and lends a shoulder
They tell me to trust in them, they understood
so don't be shy
They said that everyone does it, don't be
ashamed and don't be afraid to cry
So I know where my tears come from... they
come from within my heart
They stem from hidden emotions that I have
kept inside the dark
At times they come from laughter, memories of
happiness
Other times they come from sadness over
bearing too much stress
But now I know not to be afraid for my friend
showed me and they cared
So in my times of need, my friends, will you
help me wipe my tears?

Letter to My So-Called Best Friend

Time and time again
Whenever you needed a friend
Remember who was there for you
When you didn't know what to do
Who held you in their arms whenever you
were down?
Who told you that you were beautiful and that
you wore a crown?
Who never talked about you behind your
back?
But you do it to me, tell me, what's up with
that?
When everyone was against you
Who was there to stand beside you?
When people threw dirt on your name
And you wanted to complain,
Who was there to keep you sane?
Tell me who is to blame
Who dealt with the heartache and pain you
caused when you took their heart away?
Who held in all their anger to spare your
feelings almost everyday?
How could you turn your back on those who
had yours?
I gave you all of my love and attention but it
seems you're craving more
I actually loved you, not just an expression, I
gave it my all
Even when you let me down, I got up to break
your fall

Why? Tell me, what's your excuse? You
claimed to have been mentally and emotionally
abused but you abuse me!
They say God's love has no end
So how could you stop loving your "best
friend"?
How could you say, "Oh you can trust me?"
But go around and spread rumors about me!
How can I trust you but my business is known
to everyone?
I asked you to be quiet and look what you've
done
Don't expect an apology because I am the one
who deserves it
And don't try to make excuses because I have
already heard it
If this is how it's going to be, then I will leave
just like that
So don't expect me to speak to you, because I
am done running back.

Grudges *Trigger Warning*

At once you said you loved me
At once you said you cared
At once, my friend, I remember you saying
Sincerely that you'd be here
When my troubles were unbearable
And I couldn't find a way to cope
But you shot a bullet through my heart like a
bolt
Filled with mistrust and you misled me
Now all I think about is what you said to me
After it all happened

Before it happened, I called you
But once again... no answer
My emotions were bouncing
Around like a dancer
Out of control
You had to be the first...
The second...
The third person I called
Before I chose to make the fall
I found out that you were at the club
Alone again with a guy
You didn't even know his name
Hearing this…. that made me cry
You could have stopped me
But I couldn't reach you
So I sit here in this bed
Halfway with my life
Holding grudges against you

Because you didn't do me right
35 pain killers
But they didn't kill my pain
 Because it hurt when
I was screaming out your name
Praying that you would
Walk through the door
And help me
Get my mind up off the floor
But you didn't
Now I'll hate you after life
Because when I needed you most
You didn't do me right

I Want Nothing More Than Friendship

In my heart security is what I long for
But now I see I want nothing more
Than what I already have from you
You see I'm tryna do me too!
So now I pay less attention to you
And more attention to me
And what I need
I guess I just needed someone to show it to me
Healing from the hurt you caused
Made me realize that I don't like the cost
Of love
I'd rather just not do it or be in it
As much love as I had for you
And all the stuff that we went through
I'm still standing strong
I didn't think I would be able to pick myself up
and move on
But when I got back on the right track it didn't
take long
I still got love for you and I think I always will
I just need the chance to let you know truly
how I feel...

Best Friends

Thank you for understanding,
thanks for being there
Thanks for being concerned when you saw me
shed tears
Thank you for laughing with me,
thank you for all the hugs
Thanks for standing by me
and showing me love
I understand that you have problems and
sometimes you need me too
Thanks for not pushing me away
and letting me help you
You wash away all my troubles,
your words are like holy water
And when you break it down to me
I don't see why I bother
letting things get to me I want to be free just
like you
The way you handle things
I want to do it like you do
You're strong and brave
and confident
these qualities I adore
And I love the fact that when we are together
it's never a bore
You're an awesome pal and you said you'd be
there until the end
Nothing more than that would qualify you as
my best friend.

Thanks

Sometimes I get so sad and lonely and wish I
had someone to hold me
And talk to about my problems
And be smart enough to help me solve them

Most people are too distracted to lend an ear
Or grab a tissue to wipe your tears

That's when I pick up the phone
Pray to the Lord that you're home
Oh! Just my luck... you're always there
With a word of concern to show that you care
You always give me your opinion
Whenever I tell you how I'm feeling
You don't tell me that I'm crazy or say that I'm
weird
You always comfort me whenever I get scared

Through our trials and tribulations I don't
want the depths of my love to be mistaken
No matter who you're with, or where you are
If you've got a problem give me a call because
even if we don't last I will always remember
my past
I'll remember those calls from beginning to end
And know that even though you weren't my
man,
you were my friend

Always

Let me just say that to be with you
There's no limit to what I'd do
If you're in jail
I'll pay your bail
To set you free
To be with me
If you're stranded with no way home
Just call me up on the phone
I'll do what I can to keep you safe
Cause in my heart you have a place
If you have the blues with no sunshine
Just ask me and I'll share mine
You can never go wrong
when you've got a friend
Especially one like me
who's there until the end

Metaphors of a Friendship

You walk up to me, my arms are outstretched
to you and you push away
As if to say, you wish not to feel my embrace
Altercations cause confusion when not placed
face to face
I tell you I love you and you don't say it back
I ask what it is
You say I'm to blame for that
I've tried until exhaustion escaped from my
lungs
To build a friendship that was destined to
become... a failure, like a half-burned house
full of memories and trials
But the dried up tears are no longer on the tiles
And on the walls engraved were our names
Now our friendship is ruined.
Who or what is to blame?
When the roof went down we tried to tile it
together but then you disappeared when came
the bad weather
We had a problem with each other but it
turned out to be the same
But before we could save it, our house went up
in flames
So I ask myself if it is time to let go and let the
memories fly
Just breathe them out and leave them with the
winds in the sky
Or should we take the reins of friendship and
maturity and show them who's boss

Tell them we can conquer and won't suffer a
loss... of a good friend
Friends will come and friends will go; but as
this happens we need to know
who's going to be in your house when it falls
and help repair it
Who understands your pain and will share it?
Who's going to be in your house in the end
Because your heart is your house
all who enter are friends

Heartbreak

The Biggest Lie

I was walking...talking on the phone with a
friend
then I saw a face that made my conversation
end...
He reached in for a hug and I hurriedly put my
phone in my pocket
Then I pretended as if I was consumed in my
homework packet
he opened up his pretty lips and said... "Do
you remember me?"
and I just looked at him, thinking, "How could
he?"
he was still talking, but I couldn't hear what he
was saying
cause my words began spraying,
I said no... "I'm sorry, I don't recognize your
name
I don't recognize your face... so you must be a
lame
I don't remember how you kissed me
or how you sounded when you missed me
I don't remember your sisters and no, I never
met your dad
you never had the chance to make me happy
so how could I be sad
I'm sorry, no, I do not remember your favorite
football team
and no, I never knew you liked your pie with
whipped cream

I do not know your favorite color, or the fact
that you like to sing
I can't remember...your touch...no...not
anything
no, I can't remember anything you ever said to
me or even reading any words
what? no... I don't remember taking any
pictures with the birds
in the zoo?
with you?
you got the wrong chick
so please sir, continue with your trip!"
he laughed and said, "I didn't ask you all of
that." and he turned and walked away
after about five steps he turned and
said..."Have a great day"
all I could say was "Yea, you too"
if only you knew
how much I DO remember
after I left in September
if only you knew how I wish I could forget
every single detail of everything you ever said
I still sleep in your shirt
you never took it from me
yes, the red one with the stripes; I think about
you every night
but I remember what you did take…
my heart
and you're walking away with it now
and I'm standing here trying to stop the tears
and trying to figure out how
it all happened

and how I managed to tell the biggest lie I've
ever told
"no...I do not love you...no, go ahead... its ok...
sure, we can be friends...we will work it out...
one day...
yea...I'm cool! I'm not crying, right?"
but what you didn't know is that I cried all day
and night
yea...I'm a big girl...I'll move on, it's no stress
And yes I forgave you, but I will NEVER forget
looking at my hand thinking I should have
grabbed your hand and never let it go
I should've held your hand forever and let my
feelings show
but now...you'll really never know...
THE TRUTH

Your Side of the Bed

Your side of the bed...got lonely and yes it got
cold...
sheets still wrinkled from stories untold...
worth telling but forgotten and pieces left out
crying and laughter... jokes but what about

uhmm...I don't know.
But...
I lay here...and the radio plays sad love songs
and it goes on ... and on...and on
and I can't take it any long-er and I start yelling
and screaming and I don't understand
why this person who was my whole turned out
to be half a man
half the man I thought he was and half of what
I know he could be
how could this person be the destruction of
me?
it stills hurts you see
to know that you will never be with me
you text and you call...just the same as
before...same nicknames and phrases
and I laugh and act like it never phases
me but then I know on the inside it kills
cause I'm pretending that all this time went
past and my heart, it was healed

but...nah. I lied.

cause your side of the bed is so cold I hate
rolling over
cause one part of me thinks this isn't over
one part of me says you're coming back
that part of me is holding my heart...cracked...
like you left it...
the footprint that was left when you stomped
on it...yup still there
and people always ask why I still care
and I honestly couldn't tell you
it's just you
I sit and I pull my hair and I grind my teeth
cause you still got this hold on me
and I hate it but I love you and this world just
keeps spinning
and now it seems like I lost...when I thought I
was winning....
but...I won't win...till...I get over it...
so I realized...I have to...get over it...
so I pick up the phone and I call someone else...
and I can hardly feel my pulse
but your side of the bed...is boring and old...
so weird looking and cold
so I called him...I called my... "friend"
so that HE could come...and make it warm
again
 now your side of the bed is no longer yours...
that side of the bed is NO LONGER A BORE...

Shoes and Spots

There is this pair of shoes that sit in front of the door...
Shoes I can't fit so I think they shouldn't be there anymore...
But yet they're there and I'm told "Don't worry, it's no big deal."
So I just go on hiding how I really feel.
That ugly ass pair of shoes that I will never be able to fill
But... again, everyone says "Girl...it's never that real"
We walk past every day and everything is perfect.
Our house is clean despite that pair of shoes that is sorta suspect...
The disputes we have last for five minutes maybe more...
But no one never leaves spirit bruised, emotions tore
Randomly after a long day I saw the shoes were moved
I kept this minor detail to myself although, I disapproved
Everything had been amazing why cause a scene?
But in the back of my mind I'll never forget what I seen
Romance and love, smiles and laughs what more could I ask for?

Until I seen the shoes were no longer by the
door
I felt the same heat in my groin as I had before
Someone had worn the shoes I couldn't fit, the
shoes that I envied
 And then replaced them the next day ever so
friendly
Who is this mystery lady who wanders in and
out of my home without a care?
This girl who takes her shoes off and just
leaves them there
At the door of your heart with her own key
Something that you hadn't yet given me
 She can come and go as she please and my
feelings aren't a concern
Crying because even though we seem perfect,
I'm still waiting for my turn...
they'll never wear out and they'll never be
removed for good...
sometimes I wonder if maybe I should.
but I know that sounds insecure
but why do they have to sit by the door...
 in my face and for everyone else to see...
 it makes me look dumb I think... I'm the only
girl that lives here supposedly.
 I say, "Babe, can you move them and you
always say 'I forgot' "
so why is there still another woman's shoes in
my spot?

Heartbreaker

If I never knew what it felt like for you to touch
me, I'd had nothing to miss...
no remembrance of your kiss...
Nothing to crave, no reason to be crazed,
if I had no idea that your energy made me
sensational and that looking into your eyes
always gave me butterflies...
There would be no reason for these tears
rolling down my eyes...
do you know how it feels to break your own
heart?
To walk away knowing behind you could
leave everything that you want...everything
that you need...
To make the decision that no more selfish acts
or harsh remarks in your spirit would breed
To look someone in the face
And see their heartbreak...
And keep walking?

No More

I couldn't hate you if I tried...
I couldn't hate you if I cried...
I couldn't hate you if I lied...
cause Ima love you until I die...

...
f*ck a love, lover baby
maybe
we should go back to the days when
we were only friends
could tell you anything when I felt it late night
convos 'til the sun rose
when you kissed me on my forehead, cheek
and my nose...
cause you thought my beauty mark
was...handsome...
boy...I got so many thoughts...and then some...
of the memories
will be stuck with me
held for ransom
...sometimes I wonder if you loved me...if your
caring was true...
I wonder how you so easily turned my skies
from dark grey...to bright baby blue...
how you could make me laugh and smile so
easy and would do almost anything
to now conversations are heavy...and only sad
songs I sing
no more best friend, or babe...no more...sun
rise in your heart...
I guess... falling in love... tore us apart...

should have just let her have you cause now I
feel the pain
that could have been avoided if I wouldn't
have fell for your games
convinced me that you loved me, convinced
me that you cared
convinced me I could be the one...but in reality
I shared...
and look who ended up getting what I hurt for
it always happens when I find something to
work for
I should have realized from the start...
shoulda never let you hold my heart...
cause once best friend turned into baby
maybe
that's when we destructed...
and maybe that's why we argue and just say
f*ck it
maybe that's why its awkward when we try to
speak
maybe that's why I feel like I'm dealing with a
grief of a lost love
The cost of friends becoming lovers
so blind in our minds and now
we've lost each other
...but it's done now...it's over.
there is no turning back.
I guess...I'll call love....'cause that's who I can
thank for that.

Contradictions

Go! And I don't care if you...
no wait!
come back!
where are you going?
I thought you said you would stay forever?
ok... it's whatever!
You can leave! I don't mind! I'm independent!
dependent on the love you give so freely....
please hug me.... but leave me alone!
WAIT! ... I need you.

It hurts my pride to say those words
and honestly, I think you know that because
you always do the smallest things
to irk my nerves
and I'm prideful, so I stand strong and let you
read my mind and I don't care how long it
takes but....
why haven't you called me yet?

I have been waiting ten whole minutes, Who
do you think you are?

Can't you see that I love you?
Don't my tears concern you?
Yea, I know... you caught me flirting; sending
heart eyes, but I promise it was nothing!
and I know I told you more lies but I swear
that was my cousin! you don't believe me?????
Wooooowwwww. That's crazy!!

Ok. Well leave. Go back to your hoes. You deserve better anyway. I'm no good. I don't even deserve you. But, just give me one...no maybe 2...well maybe just give me another year to prove I can be all that you need! I just love to hear you breathe...will you marry me? I mean like, not now maybe in like five years... I still got some things to figure out but you know this is forever! I would never do anything to hurt you. Again. Look...I said I was sorry what more do you want; I'm trying! If you could be a little more patient and I know I said this last time, but this time I really mean it.

This is my heart battling with my ego.
My mind battling between my love for you
and my love for me. I'm torn between my
wants and my needs
and social media feeds
me pictures that look nothing like ours and so I
want to repaint it until I realize we will never
be perfect. I'm not even built to be a housewife!
Kanye is crazy for Kim
and Gucci may have been cloned but Keisha
still loves him
and we are still just human.

It may be too much to ask
for forgiveness from a heart you didn't break
asking you to bear with fears you didn't create
and I know at times it's too much to take the
up and downs and twist and turns but in and

out and through and through, I swear I love you...I know it's hard to understand but promise it's harder to admit that I'm sorry. That love has always hurt me so running is my default and its selfish I know, but I have to protect the greatest piece of me; my heart.

You Can't See Me

I mean you are looking at me and you could
reach out and touch me but you can't and
never have really seen me
You see what I've shown you or have you
really? You've seen the actions but never
inquired or cared about the intent behind them
because you have only ever cared about what's
behind me ...my past
And you've never quite really allowed me to
grow
Or show
You who I am. Who I've had the potential to
become. Have you heard me? Or should I call
you society because you label a young black
woman expressing her feelings and emotions
as nagging and dramatic, confidence and
bragging and label me fanatic...Ms.
attitude...that's how you see me I am young
black and gifted but you see me as loud and
BLACK and you turned me into what YOU
wanted me to be. It wasn't optional. You told
me what it was.
You are not love.
You are not gentle and not kind...you love to
plant seeds in my mind
and yet you do not even offer water to
replenish after you've drained all of my
sources of energy...oxygen...
You don't see the trauma; we can't bring up
abuse

we have to mask the scars,
we cannot tell our truth
so...what's left of me to even see?
It doesn't matter.
You couldn't see me when I was whole,
and even less now that I am broken.
No hand held out to help when you know I'm
choking
on my own fears,
my own pain,
my mistakes yet again...
You can't see me
I mean you're looking at me...and you could
reach out and touch me
but...you can't..
and never have . . . really seen me...

Uninvited

I feel like he made me open my heart to him and I gave him a spare key because I trusted him inside of it. He came in and invited all of his fears with him.

They all were living in my heart together like unwanted cousins or roaches. I didn't know anything about them. Once he got comfortable, he invited new friends over. Jealousy on one arm and neglect on the other.

They sat on the couch watching Netflix and YouTube. They cooked dinner together and took turns spending time. He spent more time with neglect because he knew it would make me anxious and chase after him for a while. He would go flipping switches in my heart like he was trying to fix an electric box.

Sending electric shock waves to my brain to make me wonder if he was cheating. Where's he at? Why hasn't he called me yet? Who else's heart does he have the key to?

From time to time he would sleep with jealousy causing him to be suspicious of me. Like really?

He said he never cared for either of them but allowed them to influence how he treated my heart. Writing on the walls felt like he was pissing on them too, cause anger and pride came to visit and he was kissing on them too. They got so close and I could feel their heat inside of me. But he still had jealousy in his ear and neglect was too. I sent fear to meet with him but it was left banging on the door.

I sent love and understanding not long after but eventually they gave up too.

Fear... love and understanding were stuck hovering outside of my heart like a forcefield waiting for him to receive them. Fear sometimes sent hate mail and love tried to get it back before he read it. But after this one time I guess it was too late.

Eventually anger and pride is who he chose to leave my heart with....leaving jealousy and neglect with me.

Rip to Love: An Ode to My Heart

I watched you destroy yourself...I stood and
watched you burn...
because I thought in my heart that it was your
turn
to die
but...something inside of me said that it may be
a mistake
decisions made by my anger and my heart full
of hate
from feelings of deceit and not feeling
appreciat-ed for so long
I just could not hold on
to this fear and this pain
it was driving me insane
and you of all things...
and your name of all words...
you of all feelings...which I never deserved

I hate you.

that's exactly what I have always
wanted to tell you.

I hate you.

and you may wonder why
and it's because you always have the tendency
to make me cry
 and when you would bruise my soul
you KNEW it you would never wipe my eyes

you hold me down and pin me to the ground
and tell me lies; of forever and ever and
promises
but never tried to make them come true!
so now I blame you… for this scar on my chest
and this glare in my eyes
those of which I could never disguise

it's your fault.

yea...you heard me.

it's your fault.

your fault that I can't move on because you
keep making me have flashbacks of previous
you's
I thought it was done and that I had paid my
dues
with my tears and my voice from yelling at the
top of it
only to be told that I was really worth-a-less
only to be held by you thinking it was comfort
- no
only to be held by you cause I had nowhere
else to go
cause you had cut off all ties to any other
emotion
…well…
you still let me hang with jealousy...
sometimes you'd let me speak to neglect

some of the friends I wanted to hang out with
their names I forget
because you kept them so distant and they
stopped caring for me because of you
because I let you control my every thought my
every move my every sight!
and I followed and believed you .. cause I
thought you were right
but no.

you were wrong.

oh so wrong.

I don't know why it took so long for me to
realize the truth about you well...
that was another friend you kept me from...
truth . . .and honesty...and trust.. and dignity..
all of these are what you stole from me
it may sound wrong but I'm as happy as can be
cause I have taken back
everything you have stolen from me
no more tears of sadness you see
cause I'm happy to say to you, Love
 R.I.P
 from here on out you are dead to me
as far as where the heart can see
you are a stranger and that's how you'll be
treated see
I have no more fight left in me
when someone comes along and appreciates
me

that's when I'll take a chance to see if it's worth
it because love, I don't deserve it
well...not you
you're the wrong kind of love
I need the strong kind of love
that kind that answers and calls and checks on
things and even if their phone never rings they
still care through it all
for better or for worse
but YOU were the worst
so though your death may be saddening
your rebirth will enlighten
because new doors will open and skies...mine
will brighten
until then...I will mourn for you

good bye my Love.

I'm Sorry I Made You Love Me.

...and then I broke you because I'm broken
And it's hard to deal with the responsibility
that comes with attachment
I knew you loved me.
In how you touched me and how you stared.
I knew you loved me. And I knew that you
cared.
Because you fought...and you argued. But you
always let me right back in with a smile and an
embrace....
Boy it was all in your face
I know you love me because it's hard for you
to speak...it's hard to reply
Because I broke you with my broken pieces but
it's not cool for you to cry
So you ignore me
I'm sorry that my broken pieces are so sharp
and my tongue is so fierce with anger of my
past and I pray that one day you let me back
in...as a friend. No...you never said that you
loved me. And yet you never needed to.
Because your love was more than words. And
your actions showed me more than I ever
needed to see. Something I admit I had never
really seen. And when we experience
something for the first time, it's scary and we
run and I thought we were just having fun...
But...
Somewhere along the line...we fell...
You in and me out...

I wasn't ready. Maybe I never really was.
And though you will never admit it...I know
that you care I just need one little favor;
although you don't owe me
I just have a request but you don't have to
show me...
Please don't hurt the next girl who wants to
love you...
And please forgive me, I'm sorry that I hurt
you.

Love Me Like You Used To

I've been wondering about something and I
have got a question for you
I have been noticing the vibes I get and they
don't feel like they used to
The times we laughed and joked and walked
around like little kids
Cuddle up on the couch and held each other,
that's what relaxing is
But after the falling out we had, it's hard for
me to change
And I don't want to be a burden, don't want to
make your life deranged
You should know how I feel
Cause I have done nothing more than keep it
real
With you...my love
For when I last looked into your eyes deep
within was painful distress
Because we're trying to work this out and
when we're apart we found that happiness...
Was less
Than it was in each other's arms
But all of this may not be true
For you
But I know how deep my love runs, deep
inside your pores
You captured my heart and kept it so let me
borrow yours
Don't push away
Unless...you just don't love me like you use to

Or maybe you're just not used to me
My silly ways and the jealousy
Which are in facts my ways of showing I care
and I adore you
Look...I want nothing more from you
But your honesty
maybe, hey, then we will see
If you really are still in love with me
I am the one that was hurt and my heart is still
wide open
I wear my badge of heartache with dignity and
pride
No matter what...I'll still love you
Even if...you don't love me like you use to

Burnt Out

I was addicted to the fire in you
But the intensity of my tears put out your
flames
Went from laughter and love
Kisses and hugs
To fighting...calling each other names...
& Like glue, I cling to the toxicity of your
"love"....
You are the object of my affection
So, I told you I wanted to feel you
That I needed to connect
You thought that meant sex
So I lied there and let you fill me
Up
And when I got up
I still felt empty.

Someone Else

It pains me to think everything
we had was a lie
It kills me to think of you
between someone else's thighs
Kissing someone's fingertips
My soul screams to think
you won't ever be mine again
Just to think
Honestly
I try not to think
Because I hate to think of you
I know that as much as I think of you and me
You're not concerned with what used to be
Like me
I hate that we had a past
& all I have from it are memories of what used
to be
When it was only me and no one else
And now there is someone getting the sweet
words of affection that I longed to hear
Someone else knows
how much for them you care
And I'm just there
Your friend
Why did it end
My heart is longing to scream out "I hate you"
with the saltiness from my tears in my eyes
Because I know deep inside that those words
are lies
We moved on to someone else's

Each for our own reasons
You out of confusion and me because I noticed treason
Within us
No trust
I try to make myself understand...and believe
that I am much better without you
But when I look at my someone else I only
think of you
And I don't want to
Because I'm trying to make my mind,
my body,
....my heart...believe that I don't love you
Not like I used to
It kills me to think that you're
not my someone else
And that I have to suck it up and move on

Life goes on
I hate having to settle for another someone else
Because I'm not yours anymore
I hate knowing you are using those eyes that I
used to love to stare
At another girl no matter who's there
Because no longer am I allowed to care
About the others that you pursue
No longer do I belong to you
Yes those eyes
That I have grown to despise
Even though we are not together
they still cause me pain
I want them to turn towards me

as you speak my name
Following I love you
Do you feel this way about me?
Or has that other someone else stolen
even that from me?

I Can Forgive, But I Won't Forget

Love me for everything I've done for you and
I'll forget everything you put me through

Love me for being your ride or die and I'll
forget how you made me cry

Love me for never leaving and I'll forget my
heart was once always bleeding

Love me for being a real true friend and I'll
forgive you, again and once again

Love me for being there any time of the night
and I'll forget that you never treated me right

Love me for believing every word you said
and I'll forgive you for always making me mad

Love me for holding it down even when you
weren't around and I'll forget that you're a
clown and forgive when you put me down

Love me for being honest, love me for being
sincere and I'll try to forget that you never
really cared

I can say that I'll forget and
I can say that I'll forgive
But the truth and the fact of the real matter is
The pain you caused is way too deep in

So I will have to forgive myself once again

for forgetting love shouldn't be painful, but
true

and forget I wasted my time with you

The Truth Will Set You Free

My friend told me this story of a girl who was
deep in love, but she ruined her whole world
She was hanging with some friends and had
way too much to drink
She was hanging with her ex that night and
didn't have time to think
She knew it wasn't justified when she realized
what she did
So many thoughts were running in circles in
her head
She had had an argument with her man prior
to this but she didn't understand or know why
it came to this
She loved her boyfriend and didn't know what
he would say
If he found out she had sex
with her ex that day...
Well I listened to the story...I
cried and this is why you see...
The girl in story...baby...it was me...

Self-Assumptions

"Who is she?"
I'm ranting and raving because I want some
answers to all the questions I've been asking
I know you got an undercover lover
Don't lie or try to disguise it
I know she exists
She calls constantly! I can't put up with this...
And I won't. I refuse.
To lose
Another heart battle
Because I put all my soldiers out there; all my
men on the line
And now you are letting someone come in and
take what is mine
I heard you say you love her
You said she was beautiful
And I can't even do a checkup she don't go to
our school
Supposedly she likes you and ya'll are always
on the phone
I wonder what you say to her when you are all
alone
You said that was your baby? Ohhh so now
that's your boo?
For the life of me...please tell me this isn't true.
I told someone to find out who it was and boy
was I surprised...
When they showed me her pictures and I was
staring into my own eyes
It was me

Paranoia and jealousy
Had made you turn away from me
So when I asked you again who it was...you
said it was nobody...
Because to you...that's who I had become.

Done Being Sorry

I've told you I'm sorry and I will say it again
Although I don't know why because you are
only my friend
I have said I am sorry repeatedly to you
But now I realize you should be sorry to
I have tried to make it right I tried to make it
better
I even broke down and wrote you a letter
On how important you are and how much you
mean to me
But like everyone else, you left me in the street
Sorting and searching through every word you
say
Thinking to myself, "Why do they treat me this
way?"
yea, I know, I know, you got your feelings hurt
But you know what, my hurting heart feels
worse
I have told you my feelings, tried to show you I
care
I see now but I didn't see before that we are
drifting apart
So, we will drift our separate ways and I will
take my broken heart
You said you fell for me and you know I fell
for you
But at this point in time, there's nothing left for
me to do, I'm done being sorry for you.

New B.A.E

I sought new love to get over the old love.
But this time, there were no dm's and date
apps,
 just journaling and a lot of naps;
a lot of prayers and a lot of tears, no exes; just
me and God.

With this new discovery, I'm changing my
number and my Netflix password. There will
be No more using me for your entertainment.

Access = denied.

So, I will need the keys to my heart back. Your
lease is up and I am afraid we won't be
renewing your contract.

I sought new love to get over the old love, but
this time, the love came from myself.

AT THE HEART OF A

Lotus

Love and Lust

Short, Sad, Goodbyes

How can I say I miss you when I cannot see
your face?
How will I ever find someone as true to take
your place
It's impossible and my heart cries at the
thought of no return
From the one and only who's perfect for me
but it's so crazy because it's you
You touched parts of my mind and introduced
me to my spirit
Helped me listen to my soul because I was far
away and couldn't hear it
To others you were strange but in those ways
you were special in my eyes because that's
how I felt around you all the time I
remember...
The times we shared though short they're so
important because it helped me to discover
what I wanted in life and helped me to find out
who I am
Through it all I found love and I never knew
what I was missing, until I found you

Confession: My Heart, My Love, My Friend

My heart was hanging off its hinges, till my
love came and broke off the rest
As many times as it has,
once again it will be put to the test
Released and unsealed,
confessions revealed
But it paid as no avail for you see I was wrong
And the wasted time I spent stressing and
restraining my words were prolonged
Emotionally I've been scarred
my heart is on the line
I'm gambling
the most precious thing I call mine
To my love whom I confessed to
I always have, and always will love you
But right now on this level our disconnection
makes me feel disheveled
It makes my heart feel cluttered with phrases,
only meant for your ears to hear
In your own words from somewhere in your
soul you uttered the words "I don't care"
How deep the pain from the shock went
trembling through my bones
Your name:, well at least in thought, I believed
I wouldn't be left alone
The tears on my pillow somehow spell your
name; the notes in the trash are connected to
you
I took the time to think I don't know what to
do; I'm still in love with you

Agape

I will love you in a way that will scare you.
I've had it be called crazy before but
technically people call things crazy that they
can't explain, they judge what they don't
understand and you don't even understand
yourself.

I will love you in a way that have you lying
awake at two am wondering where you see
yourself in five years and I will have you
tossing and turning into the night
contemplating when you shed your last tear
or the last time you felt...loved.
When was the last time someone held your
hand and said it will be ok and stayed until
those words were true?
The last time someone noticed you were
starving and fed you with emotions and
cooked you a meal that your heart yearned for?
When was the last time you felt appreciated?
And the feeling of being vulnerable scares you.
The feeling of somebody knowing your flaws
and leaving has left you traumatized; so when
I look in your eyes, I see nothing.
Not pain, not heartache.
Not happiness.
Because you are void of emotion.
But my love will wake up the feelings you
were trying to hide from.

You will have to face the demons inside of
yourself and be honest with who you really
are.
& yea that's scary.
I will push you past your limit and help you to
discover your truth.
And I pray that when that time comes,
you will love me this same way too.

Silly

I realized That I don't want to look into anyone
else eyes but yours

I don't want to kiss anyone else's face, or feel
any embrace but the one that you possess

I now confess:
I would rather cry because I miss you
Than cry from the thought of never
being able to kiss you
I would rather wake up in the morning
with a smile upon my face
Knowing that God has given me
serenity and grace by placing you in my life

I would rather fight and argue with you
If at the end of the day you still say
I love you
And because I still know what's really in your
heart is something special and kind,
something hard to find
Even in you because you hide

I want to only hear I love you babe
Then to hear all the bull from these other lames
Who tries to offer me the world
Want me so desperately to be their girl
Me and them is the answer to their math
But what they don't know
is with you in my life the world I already have

I love you beyond explanation as much as I try
to deny it
It shows when I speak and through my eyes
there's no way I can hide it
We are friends now
and friends we shall remain
Deep down inside I know you feel the same
You still care I know it's still there
You don't even have to show it
I'm glad my heart caught up with me
before it was too late
No matter how you feel I can't help but wait

Never Again

Your name I won't mention
But just pay attention
I'll just call you memory
Because that's what you gave to me
I never had no one listen to me... no actually
LISTEN to me, like you
And respond to what I say so real and so true
Long distances were a problem
But somehow someway you solved it
You found me unexpectedly I admit
But when I looked into your eyes my heart was
sent adrift
Never again did I dream that I would hear
your voice pronounce my name
But when I did I thought it must be a game
Years have passed
and thoughts of you were around
But your presence, was nowhere to be found
For a while I let go
If this was so you would come back to me as
easily as I set you free
We shared something simple
but in the heart and in my soul it was treasured
How long I had thought of you the time period
wasn't measured
I heard you on the radio and thought it was
just a thing
A guy who liked my poetry, could write, and
sing

They come and go or maybe that's just what
I've been taught to believe
What brought you back to me
I will never understand
But stepping out of my dreams
to be in front of you, man, my heart just ran
You reached out
and caught it; and stuck it in your pocket
The vibe you sent me
and how you read me with your eyes
as I think about it
I was totally surprised
But you're here now that's all that matters
Along the way we have both had our
individual struggles
Life has through us some mind consuming
puzzles
But once again we have found each other
We can do this together I feel this is forever
What's going to happen I really don't know
But one thing I do know is I
 refuse to let you go

Literacy

One day I'll meet a man who loves to read

He will pick up this book that is me.

He will indulge in every word and break down every metaphor and he will finish.

Once he gets to the end, there may be a tear in his eye or a lump in his throat but he won't put the book back on the shelf, he will carry it with him forever near his heart.

He will love to go back and learn new ways to understand the sentences in the pages and read between the lines.

He will embrace going back through the pages even when the words are faded he still remembers them...tear stained or ripped, he will still read and continue to repaint the pictures he created in his mind with only the words given to him in a book that many would have just thrown away a long time ago...

Pretender

I don't want to pretend to not love you
to get you to stay
I don't want to pretend to not love you
but it's these games you like to play
Like who will call first
And who can do the most dirt...
and clean it up quicker
I don't want to hurt you
and pretend to be happy
because you get a rise out of conflict
I don't want to chase you for your attention
because I really don't need it

Because I don't really need you...
I'm choosing to love you
I'm pretending that I don't because you like it
When I call too much you hate it
when I don't call at all you're tweaking
Never hearing a word
unless you're missing my touch
or you're lonely on the weekend
I don't want to pretend
to not love you to get you to love me
So we are both pretending
lying to ourselves because we are scared
But love...
true love cannot exist
in the same place as fear...
just let me love you...and stop pretending....

Unapologetic

I apologized...
I said I'm sorry...
And for what you will never know the reason
So many unexplained actions...and for those
you'll never know the meaning
This wasn't us
I wasn't you
It grew from lust
It wasn't true
You held me DOWN
but I needed you to UPLIFT me
You and this facade?
believe in that?
you can miss me...
never handed me a CROWN ..
just dicked me down and kissed me....
I rocked out when I deserved better...
cried when I deserved more...
The lessons that you tried to teach me left
every time I exited the door...
You were just fun for now....
And I'm sorry for believing I could be you...
I cannot ..be... a man.
I can't love and lust you in the midnight hours
and leave you without a notice
I can't come(cum) whenever I want,
roll this and blow this...
Naw...
I can't be you.
And it left you angered . . .

and emotional.
Those facts will never be admitted.
That I hit it and quit it because as a woman
I'm not allowed...right..
Because YOU too have feelings.
Right?
I promise
I loved you.
I just didn't know how....
Then....

Crush

...You're online!
Then, just like that, you go offline.
well I'm glad...
because there are so many things that have
been flowing through my mind
thoughts of so many different kinds
and every single time
I catch myself and I say...
damn....
there he goes
and it keeps me on my toes
filled with anticipation
cause I know he will never know
I've been waiting to see his name...
he'll never know I feel the same...
that honestly.
I get scared to send a message...
honestly...
I haven't been too honest...
with myself...
first conversation yea sure he made me
laugh...
but things began to change that day
he walked past....
and I knew it was him
and to myself I said...THERE HE GOES!!
but...I didn't stop you...
no...that's not my type of thing.
I pretended not to care...
well it wasn't pretending because I didn't..

then
but now...
it's so different
and it's so odd
because I catch myself thinking about you
when I don't even know WHY
and I look to the sky and think
if I had the chance to stare into his eyes
I would...
but no... I probably wouldn't.
children dream....
and it's a selfish thing to put someone on a
pedestal in your mind when you know that
they just might not live up to those standards.

but ... we do it and maybe I blew it by allowing
you to go.
well...
I ain't want him to think I was weird, or
creepy...
and to think of it now it's funny to think I care
about someone who probably
doesn't even know that I do
I hate wondering what more there is to you
I wanted to ask about everything you've been
through but I didn't...
instead every time we have spoken
afterward...I smiled.
Every time it feels like it's been for a while..
cause really I've been waiting for the smile to
come from you
so give me the chance to talk with you

walk with you
connect and breathe
listen and read you.. with you.. by you...
hmmmm.
honestly... I haven't been honest.
and honestly..
I would never actually tell you this.
that I have thought about your kiss
and how it would feel to look into your eyes
and be held by you while looking at the sky...

yea I thought of it
no like seriously...
and honestly.. I haven't been honest but now
I've let my feelings show...
yes...
I have a crush on a boy I don't know yet...
I'll continue to admire from the internet....

Real Love

We have been through so much together
And I feel that we will be friends forever
You were there when I needed a friend
And the advice you gave had no end
I feel like I have known you my whole life
With you beside me I know I will be alright
We have experienced love laughter and tears
We have shared feelings, advice and fears
We have talked about death life and
friendships
We listened to each other's views on
relationships
Together we learned to negotiate and
compromise
And how to love someone for what's inside
I have learned enough to last a lifetime
You have shown me that things in life take
time
I have learned to care; I have learned patience
and how to speak my mind
I have learned that with guys there is no rush
and I can take my time
I now know what it feels like to have someone
truly have my back
And it is you that I would truly like to thank
for that
From this point on and in the future I want you
to know this
Always and forever thank you for showing me
what true love is

Inside an Empath's Mind

There were many nights I lied awake and just
stared at you
many nights that I held you and cried...
I cried because I could feel your pain running
through my veins
YOUR pain ran through ME
and so I let the tears flow because yours
couldn't
and in those moments I fell deeper in love with
you.
I loved you because your pain felt familiar
and deep down a part of me thought that
maybe just maybe if I could heal you...
then some way...I would be healing me too...

Secret Keeper

I can't explain my emotions
My mind is constantly going
I don't know what to do
Because I am so in love with you
I can't tell you how I really feel
Although I said that I would keep it real
But this is severely deep
A secret I'm going to have to keep
I don't know if you feel the same way as I do
That's why I am hiding my feelings from you
We have been friends for awhile
So please someone tell me how
My feelings somehow have drastically grown
I am afraid of the next time that we will be
alone
If you found out how would you react
After so many months of having each other's
backs
Am I allowed to feel like this?
Am I allowed to long for your kiss?
I will keep my secrets until I am ready
Or until I know my heart beat is steady
I have got my heart under lock and key
And you are the only one who can set me free

Love.

Love.
does it have a definition or does everyone have
their own?

If the latter is true then I will share mine.
Love...is not just a word but an action and it
shines through when showing the ultimate
passion.

Love...is what we make with someone who
shares it, mutual...

Love...it's a four letter word, but it means so
much more. There are different kinds of love,
but only one can be guaranteed. The love we
get from the Father above us is unconditional
and we are still focused on getting love from
the mortal man which can be fake.

Sometimes this word can end in heartbreak.
Don't say it if you don't mean it,
you don't mean it if you can't show it
actions speak louder than words.

Never A Minute Too Late

I think about you all day
and I can't make it stop
I feel I am losing a piece of you
with every teardrop
I can't predict the next time we will be together
And my feelings change just like the weather
One day I am determined and full of hope
The next day I am crying
and my pillows are soaked
No one will, or understands the way I feel
No one believes that what we have is real
You are the one I always confide in
If I need you to,
you would stay up and talk to me
You never had a problem with the things I did
You always put up with me
when I acted like a kid
You said that for me you would always wait
And when I call
you'll never be a minute too late
You told me destiny brought you to me
And that's the way we want it to be

Love for Always

It's been hard since we have been apart
And somehow,
someway you have made it back in my heart
I spent long days remembering the times
we have had
Going through the motions,
the good and the bad
Sometimes my last nerve is what you get on
But I tend to miss you whenever you are gone
Although we didn't make it
My love for you never faded
Seeing you all the time
made my heartbreak worse
I used my happy attitude to cover up the hurt
Love is what I believed we would have forever
In my heart I believed we would be together
In love for always
until we did part
Will you please
help me mend my broken heart?

It's as If....

I missed you...
no… for real...I really missed you
my heart was reaching out to you
But the distance was so far that we could not
exchange the emotions, feelings and words
pumping from our blood in our heart to the
vessels in our brains.
I missed you as if I would never see you again
and I am alone to weep and wonder
If there will ever come another like you.
It's as if the sun set on our love and will never
rise again,
I need to be reassured that you will not be long
gone
when I return in the mornin' after I had
already left.
I missed you.
I missed you as if I were a star, but then the
clouds came and I realized it was time to let
you go
For my shine was just a show that had to end
so now I have to let you know how I really feel
While in your embrace
I remember missing you
Fantasizing about kissing you
Dreaming of watching the stars with you
Making ideas go so far with you I wanted to
While I was missing you I thought about doing
all of the above with you
I suddenly realized I am in love with you.

I Loved You.

At least....
I thought I did.
I dreamt of you;
memories laced with your smile haunt my
sleep.
Adornment in the purest form.
But your absence escaped me...
& I waited...patiently.
I loved you.
And you loved me back...when it was too late.

Only If

Only if it was you and me
Only if it could be just we
Only if you could hold me now
Tell me stories and explain to me how a love
like this could be found
If my mom could see she would be so proud
Only if we could run away; find a faraway
place to stay
Only if we could fly
If we could run out of tears to cry
Only if we could watch the stars, or go to mars
We could watch people on earth live their
tragic lives nut we would be together
it would be just right
Only if we never had to worry about words
violence and death
Everyone disappearing; we would be the only
ones left… to start a new world baby it would
be up to us
Only if we could be together from dawn till
dusk
If I could find someone like you
Who treats me like you do
I want you to know that I am always here
You are on my mind and I will always care
Only for you do I want these things
For you I want the good that life brings
I want to be there for you when you need me
Only if I could hear you say you believe me

Only if our dreams came true; Only if I gave
my heart to you

Nature's Intuition

Calm winds
Summer nights
How the birds sing
The beauty of the sunlight
How I feel when I'm with you
How you keep me safe and warm
How you give me inspiration
How your words keep me strong
How I tell you all my secrets
And you know how I feel
And how the love you have for me
How I know that it's real
The movements of the clouds
The rhythm of the trees
How the look in your eyes
Is the only look for me
Oh, how it makes me feel so special
Like I am the only one
Who can see the birds, trees and clouds
And see the beauty of the sun

Heart for Sale

He said, "This is all I have to offer,"
& handed her his heart.
She looked inside and saw it was damaged.
But also that it was missing some things.
There was no consistency,
no integrity....
no stability of any kind.
She scoped the bottom to see if she had missed
the commitment.
Went deeper to see if she could find honesty.
There were some red flags but she shuffled
through those because communication, passion
and romance were sprinkled throughout.

She asked, "How am I supposed to make this
work? I don't see any drive or ambition in
here?" She sighed, & handed his heart back.
She said, "This was nice of you to offer...
but unfortunately, I can't do much with that."

And she turned and walked away.

"Over time, I have realized how much HEALING is done in the dark. Although invisible to the human eye, GOD STILL SEES ME."

~Starr

www.ingramcontent.com/pod-product-compliance
Lightning Source LLC
LaVergne TN
LVHW011332080426
835513LV00006B/302